My Dog.

One day we found a dog in our garage. So we gave her five pieces of bologna six pieces of bread 1 can of cicle 8 two like she hadn't ate for a very long time. She had no colar so we kept the dog we named her Foxy. She is white and she's a Sips, she looks like a samoyed but she's not.

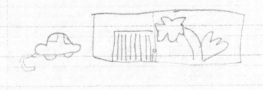

My house.

One day the movers came to take our furture to Houston in Denver Colo. My mommy picked a house with a Iron gate a bathroom in every room with no stairs, a small back yard big frount yard & five court yards including the back yard, 3 rooms, a water founton inside, and old fashion fan in the same room. and soon we will have a 2 story house same house. we will make it!

COOKIE SALES

*H*ouston, *1978.* I am ten. We are in someone's den, brown shag carpet with snacks on the table. My mother is in the hallway telling the leader of Brownie Troop No. 13 that while I did not sell enough cookies, my family should not have to make up the difference. Maybe I was too scared to sell, or maybe I forgot, or maybe we didn't think they would actually hold us to it. As my mother argues in careful English, I feel the other Brownies' eyes on me. None of us eat. I am embarrassed by the scene my mother is causing, wishing I could disappear. I am the only Asian Brownie for miles, though I don't understand yet what this means.

It would continue like this for several years—me underselling cookies, me embarrassed by my mother, me wishing I could disappear. I stuck with Girl Scouts even when we moved to Hong Kong. I was a Cadette by then, and just starting to understand how you could still be on the outside even in a place where the majority of people looked like you. "TOFS" was the new badge I got to put on my sash, for "Troops on Foreign Soil" which made me wonder. Because who, really, was the foreigner?

GRAVE

For four weeks in the summer of 1983, I went to live with my aunt I-An and her family in Taiwan. I-An was my father's younger sister. I was a fourteen-year-old Chinese American kid living in Hong Kong, clueless about the proper way to address our many different aunts, uncles and cousins. I held my chopsticks splayed, didn't speak much Chinese, made a face when things seemed strange or weird. I shook my head when offered a piece of prickly fruit I didn't recognize. I was hopelessly American, and I knew it.

The problem was, so did everyone else.

My mother decided to go on a four-week spiritual retreat in Crested Butte, Colorado. My father was traveling between Hong Kong and the States. My younger brother was at summer camp somewhere on the East Coast. I was not old enough to be trusted alone in our apartment in Hong Kong, where we were living as expatriates. They needed to put me somewhere, with someone who could handle me and my challenging, often exhausting behavior.

When I arrived in Taiwan, my cousins stared at me. My uncle didn't speak English. I forgot everyone's name within minutes of being told who they were. I was too embarrassed to ask again and tried to figure it out when I heard my aunt addressing them at dinner.

After a few days, I-An took me to the grave of my grandmother, a woman I met only two or three times before she died. I called her *Năi Năi*, the proper address for a paternal grandmother, but I was confused. I thought the word *năi* meant *breast*. I didn't know then that Chinese characters could sound the same, save a slight inflection, but have different characters and different meanings.

During one of those early visits when she was still alive, I whispered this question to my mother—why did the words for grandmother and breast sound alike? My grandmother overheard, and she laughed, delighted. "Because they both give milk!" she said, in Chinese or stilted English, I don't remember. I blushed a furious red as the adults chuckled. When I studied Chinese in college, I leaned that the character for paternal grandmother was the same character as the one for breast—the same tones, the same strokes. I thought she had been making a joke, but my grandmother had been right.

In the States, we had driven past graveyards numerous times, and for the few years we lived in Hong Kong, we would pass cemeteries stacked up on the mountains, each headstone a price tag and crammed tight since real estate was at a premium. "Hold your breath!" my brother and I would tell each other, in case wandering spirits slipped in. I would do this for years, even when I went to boarding school. Not far from campus was a cemetery, and I would walk by the tall and narrow headstones, worn with time and weather. I tried not to think of skeletal arms reaching out to grab me. I would suck in my breath until I passed.

There was protocol for paying respects to a dead relative, but I didn't know what it was. I figured it would be like the movies—incense burned at the base of the graves, kowtowing, chest beating, a full spread of food and paper money, that sort of thing.

"We don't do that," my aunt told me briskly. They were Christian. Traditional Chinese rituals were considered superstitious and old fashioned. I don't remember flowers but there must have been some. I'm sure my aunt bought a bouquet and handed them to me to place on the grave, as if my grandmother wouldn't notice I hadn't bought them myself.

There was no escaping the heat. Every direction I turned for relief only offered more of the same, an impenetrable wall of hot, wet air. It was humid, typical of a Taiwan summer. My best bet was to stay still, to breathe as little as possible. I wished I could sit down, even if it meant leaning against a tombstone. Instead, I halfheartedly cleared some brush away from the grave, feeling like I should at least try to be a good Chinese granddaughter. It wasn't much, but it was all I had. When I was finished, I didn't know where to put the dead branches, so I held them in my hand like an offering and waited for my aunt to finish whatever she was doing.

I wanted air conditioning. I wanted to go home.

But no one was home. There was nowhere else for me to go, no one else who would take me. So I stood there, sweating in the bright sun until my aunt started to walk away, and called for me to hurry along.

HALLELUJAH

I grew up alongside collection plates at the Baptist church of white people near our house and then at the Baptist church of Chinese people across town. Clutching coins and dollar bills, waiting for my turn, the anticipation making it impossible to hear what the pastor was saying. Hell? Brimstone? Love thy neighbor? Who knows. After a few years, my parents stopped taking us to church. My brother and I didn't bother to ask why.

. . .

In middle school, I found Jesus again, hands in the air as people around me spoke in tongues. When I was baptized, the gown was heavy. The lukewarm water in the blue-tiled baptismal pool was gross. I stumbled when I emerged, wondered if it was a sign.

. . .

At night, I heard unborn babies crying.

. . .

I refused to look in the mirror after watching *The Omen*, fearful of a spectral noose around my neck. I bought boxes of evangelistic tracts with titillating cartoons depicting every manner of sin, making sin look pretty appealing, if I'm going to be honest. I told my father he was going to hell. He was reading the newspaper and didn't look up, said, *Oh well.*

· · ·

Once I felt an evil presence outside my bedroom door.

· · ·

In college, I dropped the church thing. I started a pro-choice group. Someone keyed my car. I still believed in God, but it was the other stuff that was suspect. Around that time, my mother converted to Buddhism. She told me and my brother she was no longer our mother.

· · ·

You can imagine how I felt about that.

· · ·

Now, at fifty, bronze Buddhas sit in my home. Sometimes I listen to Joel Osteen. For a few years I streamed videos of Abraham, a group of spiritual entities channeled through a woman named Esther. I know it sounds like I'm covering my bases—does that make me less of a believer? This isn't the pandemic talking, but if ever there was a time to declare your faith, this is it. So here is mine.

I still pray. I have seen miracles happen in my own life. More than once, I have felt a calming, divine presence. I believe in karma. Maybe reincarnation. I do not think we are alone in this world. I believe there is *more,* that there is *something out there,* and that it is *greater than us.* I yearn for kindness, in my own life and in others. I hope to live in a way that invites joy, freedom, peace.

This is my prayer.

LEAVING

My mother and I are having tea in the basement of the communal Buddhist house where she has lived for the past thirty years. She converted to Buddhism in her fifties, ten or so years after my brother and I boarded planes for separate boarding schools on the East Coast.

"I want to thank you," she says. "For going away."

There is a prickle at the back of my neck. The topic of boarding school has always been one we've never really discussed. I keep my voice even. "What do you mean?"

She gives a tired smile. Her grey hair is cut short, the skin on her face pale and soft—she is in her early eighties. In this smile I see distance, discomfort, guilt, relief. "I couldn't handle you or your brother," she tells me. "I needed space. I needed you to go."

"Okay," I say, but of course it's not okay. She needed us to go? It wasn't about setting us up for life, college prep, more opportunities, et cetera, et cetera?

"Your father was having an affair," she says. She stops and corrects herself, sighs. "Maybe it wasn't an affair. Maybe they were just friends, but I was jealous. Things had not been going well for a while. I had been on a trip to Taiwan to visit relatives. The minute I walked through the door you told me what happened—she had been in our apartment. You were angry. You wanted me to know."

I do not remember this. I travel back the thirty-some years to my teenage self. My father, his business trips, my mother's loneliness. Story and memory run together. It's hard to remember what was real.

"It was easier for me when the two of you left," she says. "You were so demanding, always fighting and argumentative. It was too much for me to do alone, taking care of you and your brother."

How might this have played out in an alternate universe? Could we have stayed? *Would* we have stayed? Could we have promised to be better children, less of an emotional drain on our mother, staying out of the business of their marriage? What kind of family might we have become? What kind of person might I have turned out to be?

The decision to send me to an all-girls boarding school in Connecticut started with a possibility. We had been living as expatriates in Hong Kong for my father's job at an oil company. There was talk about moving us to a part of mainland China where no English-speaking school existed. My brother and I were of Chinese descent, but we did not speak Chinese fluently. We were ABCs—American-born Chinese, also known as bananas—white on the inside, yellow on the outside. Four years in our expatriate enclave did little to build any new language skills. We could swear and we could order food. That was it.

Every catalog featured the same leafy campus, leggy brunettes carrying armfuls of books, tow-headed jocks brandishing lacrosse sticks, the occasional Asian student with a cello propped between her legs or leaning over a microscope. The teachers wore cement-colored corduroy pants, thick-cabled sweaters, wire-rimmed glasses. Their faces channeled focus and commitment as they made a grand gesture toward their students. I knew I would never fit in. I had nothing in common with these kids, who were smart or privileged or talented. I wasn't even there and already I felt like a fraud.

Then the news came: we would not have to move to China after all—my father would commute. But things progressed as if nothing had changed. My brother and I sat for the PSAT, flew to the East Coast to tour campuses, applied to a bunch of schools, got into a few. There was no *Why are we still going?* or *Can we stay?* If that had been a possibility, I wasn't aware of it. Instead we dutifully said goodbye to parents and friends, packed our bags and left.

At the airport, my brother and I went our separate ways, him to Massachusetts and me to Connecticut. We would never live under the same roof again.

In 2011, psychotherapist Joy Schaverien published an article in the *British Journal of Psychotherapy* and introduced the term "Boarding School Syndrome." It was used primarily to identify lasting psychological problems in adults who were sent away to boarding school at a young age, usually during elementary or middle school. I was a sophomore in high school in 1984 when I went to Connecticut. Did this "syndrome" apply to me?

After boarding school, I went to college. During my sophomore spring, I moved back to Houston and transferred to a local university. My mother had repatriated while my father continued to work overseas. I was sleeping in the room of my childhood, the same pink-flowered bedspread, the same kid-sized white laminate desk. At that time I told myself it was for practical reasons. Why spend money on rent when I could live at home?

I told myself the same thing when I went to work overseas with an international tax firm. The chairman of our China practice said he would hire me, but I wouldn't have benefits like housing.

"No problem," I said, because I had a place to stay. My father was living in Beijing, his apartment on the same street as our office. I would stay with him.

In both cases my parents hadn't agreed to let me stay with them. It was more like they didn't say no, and before they could gather their thoughts, I was unpacked. My mother tolerated it longer than my father. After a year, he told me I had to leave.

I was defiant. How could he kick me out? *I was his daughter.* It didn't matter that I was also a professional woman in her mid-twenties who made her own money and could afford a place of her own. That wasn't the point.

Except it *was* the point.

I was trying to throw myself back into the nest. I didn't know that then and could only feel the raw hurt of being told I needed to go. I hadn't been ready to leave when I was fifteen, and I was trying to reclaim those lost years with my parents. But it was too late.

I moved out. My father and I assumed the relationship of two adults who lived in the same city but were too busy to see each other.

One day I walked into the lobby of the Beijing Hotel to meet a friend for brunch. There was my father, sitting in a chair in the lobby and reading the paper. We startled when we saw each other, as if we were the last person we ever expected to see. Then I was overcome with what I can only describe as elation and joy, of relief at seeing this man who was my father.

"Daddy," I said. My voice broke—you'd think it had been years rather than weeks since I had last seen him. I gave him a long hug.

"*Xiao Yi*," he said, calling me by my childhood nickname. He smelled as I remembered—his skin, his clothes—the solidness of my father hadn't changed. My eyes filled with tears. He hated tears—it made him uncomfortable, so after a few seconds, I stepped back. We both had places to be. A small distance formed between us. It made it easier to say goodbye.

AT THE AMERICAN CHAMBER OF COMMERCE DINNER IN BEIJING (1995)

We wait for our dinner at linen-draped tables. Side by side, we smile at one another. The woman could be from Iowa or Colorado or Montana or California. Her name might be Evelyn or Florence or Charlotte or Carol. We are in China, a country of one billion Chinese faces. She says, *I have lived here for six years, I feel almost local.* She sees these faces every day—Chinese people walking along dusty sidewalks, Chinese people working in her home, Chinese people driving her from Point A to Point B. It took a long time to learn their names. She laughs, *It's too easy to mix them up.* She gave them American names or truncated their Chinese ones—Johnny, Xiao Hu—or called them by their job titles—*sījī* for driver, *āyí* for maid. Her husband works for Shell Oil Company. I am young, twenty-six, Chinese American, born in St. Louis, raised on Wonder Bread and Hershey's. "But still," the woman says. She pats me on the arm, leans in close. "Your English is so good."

RICHES

What we did was argue first—eat now or eat later? On the train to Chengdu or when we pulled into the station in Taishan? At one stop, I opened the smudged pane window and leaned out, waving a ten-*yuan* note. What did we get? Steamed buns, chicken, rice, soup? We knew what every dish was called, we knew what to ask for—parsley, pickled vegetables, hot sauce, no egg. We had crumpled bills of five-*jiao* or ten-*fen* notes that we tossed into the basket with the others, stood alongside the local Chinese as we waited for our food with feigned impatience, feeling like we belonged.

For street crepes, we knew not to inspect the containers too closely for anything floating in the batter. For noodles, we averted our eyes from vats of steaming but not boiling water that could harbor something most Westerners would try to avoid. We were here for work, the expatriates and me, the token Chinese American. Some of us had better Chinese than others. We delighted in the surprise of the locals—not the sophisticated Beijingers—who shared their smokes and engaged in conversation, their accents so thick we didn't know what they were saying. We nodded our heads anyway. We bought them beer, made friends for the hour.

We played Uno in the waiting areas of planes, trains, buses. Is it sentimental to say these were the best days of my youth? Roaming the country as if we owned it, knowing full well we were guests that wouldn't be asked to leave. Not us. We got it.

Our travels gave us stories to tell. They made us interesting, worldly, and only occasionally would someone appear who was the "real thing." American or European, fluent in several languages (English, French, German, Dutch), but especially in Chinese, maybe Mandarin or Cantonese, plus a random but enviable dialect they learned "for fun" like Shanghainese. They were well educated, Ivy League in the US, Oxford or Cambridge in the UK. They were stylish, impeccably dressed, no matter if it was hot or sticky or humid. They exuded an air of affluence and coolness, as if they'd stepped out of a Merchant Ivory film, linen whites rumpled in just the right places. They had better jobs, private cars, a black-suited driver. Designer dress bags or roll-on suitcases that mysteriously fit all their amazing clothes and polished shoes.

They had fiancés, an apartment paid for by the company, a vacation planned in Bali (Four Seasons Jimbaran Bay or Amandari). A provincial part-time villa in Europe, an annual ski trip in the Alps. They always looked good, never beaten down from this country because they were just flying in for a bit—

we were the suckers on the ground. They would give us backhanded compliments. "It's amazing what you do—I could never live here full-time. I'm just not built that way." How were we built? What kind of animals were we?

You could see our cracks if you looked close. We didn't negotiate low enough at the silk market, we were taken for a ride with the fake antiques. Sometimes we pushed into crowds and felt utterly alone. The workmen in our apartment buildings were slow to fix our showers/stoves/heaters. Why should they be at the beck and call of these young foreigners? Still, we always found a way. We showered at the gym, grabbed breakfast on the way to work, dinner on the way home from the office. We could layer up in the winter—Ralph Lauren or Burberry knock-offs were cheap and looked like the real thing. We could do this like no one else, bask in our own fame and fortune, tell ourselves, *this is the life*. We were young. We had nothing to lose.

EXPATRIATE

1.

At the airport, I look at my passport, check my wallet for money, see both USD and RMB. In front of me, a wall of Chinese faces and above them a sign, *Beijing Welcomes You*. People squeeze into any empty space, stand pressed behind an uninterested guard who seems no more than seventeen years of age. A white couple walks by and the crowd comes to life, signboards at attention for a "Mr. Benn" or "Motorola Co" or "Great Wall Sheraton Hotel." Men with smoky voices point to the darkness outside, grasp an invisible steering wheel, pretend to drive. *Taxi, you want taxi?*

2.

Felicity is from the UK, grimaces at the porridge in front of us. It tastes bland, like paste. I reach for the pickled cabbage with my chopsticks. Felicity shakes her head, wipes the rim of her teacup with a tissue. "I don't know how you can eat that," she says. "It must be in your genes."

3.

My boss lives in Building 3 in the diplomatic compound. With the strap of my briefcase slung across my body, I inch forward, know my business suit does not fool the guard. He stares straight ahead, expressionless, but as I am about to pass, he steps in front of me with his rifle. He barks in Chinese that I am not allowed inside. Anger bubbles up, words spilling from my mouth in clear, privileged asshole English. "I'm American!" I wave my passport in his face. The guard is quick to apologize, confusion on his face. I breeze past him then slow with each step, feeling as if I have left something at the gate.

4.

After introductions, the government official in charge of the project reads my business card, printed on one side in Chinese, the other in English. "Where are your parents from?" he asks me in Mandarin. I tell him their home provinces, hoping he will be impressed with what I know. He stares at me hard. "You act so American, you should be ashamed. You are Chinese!" My American colleagues shuffle around, wanting to know what he said.

5.

On a long-distance call from New York, my cousin says, "Come on, I'm paying for this call. Speak some Chinese." I offer a few phrases. *How much for those slippers? Where is the toilet? I'm a vegetarian.* He laughs at my Americanized accent. "My Chinese is better than yours, and I've never even been there!" His voice breaks up over the telephone line.

6.

The client is frustrated, complains about the Chinese workers in his office in Wuxi. *They're lazy,* he tells me. *They want salaries like expats. The women even get paid time off for having their period!* I listen and nod, keep it professional. When he leaves, I am surrounded by the local girls in my office, mostly secretaries, who giggle and loop their arms through mine. They lead me to the food court, asking questions in slow, careful English, about America and will I write them when I leave.

7.

One Sunday in May, I wander around Tiananmen Square, watching people fly kites. I look up at the sky and see colorful dragons and solemn Mandarin officers, attacking owls and hawks. Everyone is out today, playing with their one child, and somehow I get swept up in a crowd running to catch a bus. They push and pull, not caring if I am Chinese or American or both or neither.

8.

At the airport, I look at my passport, check my wallet for money, see both USD and RMB. In front of me, a wall of Chinese faces. People squeeze into any empty space, stand pressed behind an uninterested guard who seems no more than seventeen years of age. They wave goodbye to friends and relatives, calling out, *Yīlù shùnfēng* — travel well with the wind behind you. They watch me as I gather my things, waiting to see where I will go.

II.

We are becoming ourselves.

—BYRON KATIE

TINY LOVE STORY

We met at the baggage claim at LAX—he was picking me up as a favor to my best friend. By midafternoon, we were holding hands. A clerk at the post office told us, "You're a match made in heaven." That evening we met up with my friend who socked him across the jaw—his glasses went flying across the dance floor at the Mayan. Turns out she liked him, too. Five years later, she and I were no longer friends. He and I found each other again, reunited in New Zealand. We moved to Hawai'i and had three kids.

NAMES FOR
DIFFICULT THINGS

My due date has come and gone. As agreed upon with my doctor, I check into our rural, thirty-five-bed hospital in Waimea, even though nothing is happening. My vitals are fine, the baby looks good. Two weeks overdue means it's time to induce, that's all.

My husband starts filming as we lug my hospital bag to the car, my belly round. I wave to the camera. He films the spacious private room of the maternity wing, its warm *koa* floors and matching rocking chair overlooking a private garden. The bed is comfortable and designed for deliveries so everything can happen in this beautiful space—I won't have to go anywhere. My husband films the clock on the wall, reporting the time, because the baby might be coming any minute.

It is like this throughout the day. We address the camera with small updates, each one shorter than the last. I am hooked up to a Pitocin drip, my contractions occasionally spiking on a monitor. Day turns into evening turns into morning, and then happens all over again. The video camera sits in our bag, the novelty of documenting every moment having run its course. Three full days in with nothing to show, not a contraction in sight.

My acupuncturist stops by and places needles on my body, opens my meridians. He has white hair and bright blue eyes, a regular at the hospital, well respected by traditional and alternative practitioners alike. I jokingly ask him what's taking so long, because, like, we have things to do.

"Honestly?" he tells us. His face is serious. "I don't think your baby's ready to come."

After he leaves, my husband and I discuss this in whispers in the bathroom—*that's it*, we agree. *She's just not ready!* The idea of heading home takes hold. We are exhausted. Neither of us have slept well. There is always someone coming or going, sounds of women and families, the metallic click of the door each time it closes. I have been maxed out on Pitocin for long stretches. The Cervidil starts contractions that go nowhere. I'm on a semi-liquid diet of Jell-O, a dinner roll and apple juice, standard protocol for laboring mothers in case they need to do a C-section, which means I'm starving.

We are buoyed at the thought of leaving and letting nature take over. Isn't that how it's supposed to be? We should be following the baby's timetable, not ours! There is no medical emergency here. The baby is fine. I am fine.

When we tell the doctor our plans, she frowns. She speaks in a slow, deliberate voice. She can't be responsible for what happens once we leave the hospital, and hints at trouble we might encounter upon our return. After all, we've been here three days, the hospital bill an open tab. She levels her gaze and my husband and I think the same thing—will she be difficult or unhelpful when we return? Am I putting myself at risk and, more importantly, our baby at risk? What kind of parents are we? This is our first pregnancy, our first baby—what do we know? Maybe she's right. The doctor waits as I go back to bed and crawl between the paper-thin sheets. She returns a couple hours later to break my water. When she ruptures the amniotic sac, the slow descent into hell begins.

Twelve hours and eight centimeters later, I have an infection and a 104°F fever. "You know what this means," the doctor says. She waits for me to say something but there is nothing left to be said. It is unlikely I will get to ten centimeters, that magic number when everything opens up. My birth plan has long gone out the window. I am not progressing. I am angry and disappointed and sad and hungry. If I had the energy, I might have screamed, but I cannot find my voice. Instead I lay there like a lump and manage an angry, defeated nod.

It is 2:00 a.m. My husband stumbles to the operating room ahead of us, the halls quiet and empty. He gives them our birth CD, a playlist of songs we listened to daily over the past few months. They are our songs—his, the baby's, mine. The first song is playing when they wheel me in. Israel Kamakawiwoʻole's "Somewhere Over the Rainbow."

I cry for them to turn it off.

What follows is an abrupt stillness. In the absence of song, I hear stainless steel instruments rattling around, muffled whispers among the surgical staff. When it's clear the epidural is not working, they decide on general anesthesia. Leather straps are slipped onto my wrists as I am belted down. They usher my husband out of the room and put an ill-fitting mask over my face. I black out.

I wake up once after the surgery in a dark room, a young nurse sitting in a chair next to me. She is reading a magazine, bored. She doesn't look up or notice I'm awake. I wait and then fall back into a well of darkness.

When my eyes open a few hours later, there is an empty bassinet next to me. I am back in my hospital room, as if I'd never left—a stream of diffused sunlight fills every corner. Outside, the trees are a verdant green. It will be eight weeks before I can drive. If I hold my breath, I don't notice the stitches pulling across my abdomen, can't feel my hoarse throat. I have to practice breathing again. Next to the window, my husband stands shirtless with our daughter pressed against his chest. He turns when he hears me stir. He whispers, "That's your mom."

He presses his lips to the whorl of her downy head. Then he crosses the room and places her in my arms. There is no denying this gentle weight against my body. Her warmth, her sweet breath. Grasping fingers that curl and uncurl as they reach for me. Her eyes glance over my face, as if she can't believe she is finally here, that we have somehow made it through.

PHOTOGRAPH: POOLSIDE SELFIE AT THE FOUR SEASONS HUALĀLAI

The four of us seated in a row—my brother, me, my sister-in-law, my husband. My sister-in-law is pregnant and my husband holds our five-month-old daughter in his lap, a portrait of two families in the making. Our bodies angle toward the camera as if this promised land will stop time from moving forward. The frame of towering palm trees and perfect blue skies evidence a holiday from life, not life itself. My brother and his wife will divorce within a year. A decade later, he and I will no longer speak. Other bodies will assume the position in these chairs. Other bodies will believe this paradise.

MULTIVERSE

My sister-in-law wants to give CBD oil to my father-in-law. She wants the cannabidiol hemp oil tincture to release him from his Parkinson's, to steady his gait and calm his quivering tongue. She wants to see the old Pa, to release him from a body, this cage of disobedient muscles and nerves. She wants to hear him talk, because we have no idea what is going on inside his head. When he does speak, we cannot understand him. Is he happy or unhappy? Is he suffering? Is he in pain? She emails us a link to a video and tells us to watch it.

. . .

We gather around his bed. *Take this*, my sister-in-law will say, and because Pa cannot say or indicate yes or no, she will place a few drops under his tongue before anyone else can say, *Stop, it might interfere with his meds, let's ask the doctor first*. Maybe. What if. We want. Our desires push against the bedrails.

. . .

If it works, what then? In the YouTube video, the man is upright and talking. *My voice is back,* he tells the camera. His name is Larry. Gone are the tremors in his hands—he holds his fingers out, flat and steady. He asks the documentary team if they've had lunch. He stands up, leaning lightly on a cane that an hour ago was his best support. He was writhing then, coiling around his own body, lips pursed around the small tube of cannibis oil, everything in motion. Now he's calm, looking around as if to say, *what's next?*

. . .

I picture Pa sitting up, as if he's woken from a nap, refreshed. He tells us he's fine. He'll thank his children for being there, the spouses and grandkids, too. He'll crack a joke. He'll greet the nurses and caregivers— *Hey there, Roger! Looking good, my friend!* He'll ask to see Betty, his wife. *Hi, honey.* They will sit together on the bed, arms looped, she perched by his side as she has been all the years of their marriage. As if nothing has changed.

. . .

He'll walk himself to the lunchroom, seat himself at the table. He will crack another joke with the waitstaff, and then say, *Keep up the good work!* He'll talk between bites, telling us what it was like. *I mostly felt like I was dreaming.* He'll ask after friends and older relatives. He'll express remorse if someone is ill or has died. *That's a shame.* He'll ask each of his kids about work, praising them, or maybe after everything he's been through, he'll give them some advice. *Spend more time with the people you love.* Since he became a Christian, he might say, *God is good. He is good.*

. . .

Instead, we do nothing. We listen to the doctors, we visit when we can. We buy children's toys for him to play with during his waking hours when he's rolled into the hallway in front of the nurses' station—a lacing board, a large wooden puzzle, a baby doll. We say, *How're you doing, Pa? What'd you have for lunch?* even though we know he can't reply. We tell him he looks good. We walk with him in a slow loop around the assisted living facility, someone on either side.

. . .

Sometimes he looks at us and everything we remember about him flashes across his face. How strict he was, how kind he was, how generous, how cheap. How he would give anything to play a round of golf (remember that hole-in-one?). How he championed Asian professors and students at Chico State University, where he taught for over thirty-five years—he was the go-to guy for anyone new, helping with applications, forms, translations. How he was clean and particular. Punctual. Disciplined. How he came to the country at thirteen with a paper name, a last name the family would legally change when my husband was nine. We would look at him and remember it all.

FLIGHT

My daughter is sixteen and on a school trip to New York City. It's a long way from our home in Hawai'i, but she's no stranger to travel. She's been abroad, both with us and on her own. This will be her third trip to New York, a city that she loves. Her demeanor and self-confidence add a couple more years—she's often mistaken for a college student, both in appearance and attitude. She is ready to fly the coop. "Bye!" she'll say cheerily whenever my husband or I bemoan the impending countdown to her departure for college in less than twenty-four months.

But this trip to New York—one in which she is the head of a Model United Nations delegation, a trip she has been looking forward to all year—is different. Winter Storm Stella has canceled more than half of the group's flights. For a while there is the possibility she might end up in New York City alone and hotel-less, but everyone eventually gets rebooked and they arrive only a few hours after her.

On the second night she breaks up with her boyfriend of two and a half years. One of the girls in her room refuses to shower. The schedule is relentless—up at 7:00 a.m., back by 11:00 p.m. She's eating food from the vending machine. She can't sleep.

She calls me at 9:30 p.m. Hawai'i Standard time, which is 3:30 p.m. in New York. She is crying.

"I want to come home," she sobs. "I hate it here. I want to be with you and Dad."

I have never heard her say these words before and for a moment I am speechless. I ask her to tell me what's going on.

She misses her now ex-boyfriend even though she thinks she did the right thing. Nobody else understands. Several people in the group have come down with the stomach flu. She still has homework. Everyone is exhausted.

There are ten days left on the trip. "Get some sleep," I tell her. "We'll talk in the morning."

But she can't sleep—she wants to talk now. I stay up with her for another hour, listening to her cry, then rant, then rage, then cry again. Sometimes it's directed at her classmates, sometimes it's directed at me ("You don't understand!"). Sometimes it's just the sound of her breath and mine. That's all.

Before we hang up, I tell my daughter if she wants to come home early from her trip, then her father and I will make it happen. We'll figure it out in the morning.

"Okay," she says, her voice quiet. The ragged crying has subsided and there is only the occasional sniff. "Okay."

· · ·

The next day when we check in, she says, "I'm fine. I guess I'll stay."

"You don't have to," I say. "I can call your teacher." We have looked into flights. I have planned how the rest of the school year will go—a new set of friends, refreshed priorities, more family time.

"You don't need to," she says. "I feel better today."

We check in daily for the rest of the trip, by phone or email or text. They're in Los Angeles now—the second half of the trip is for a robotics competition. New drama has surfaced and just as quickly subsided. Every time I offer an out—to come home, to break from the group and stay with relatives—she chooses to stay where she is. It takes me a while to realize that she is not coming home, not yet, that coming home was never the issue. She is doing what children do—growing up, testing their wings. My own upbringing has impacted the way I parent—either/or, fight or flight.

I busy myself with other things, counting the days to her return. There is nothing to worry about, nothing to mourn. But I worry and mourn just the same, because I am doing what parents do—growing up. Learning to let go.

BANQUET

Qingdao, China. I try to see myself in their faces, these relatives on my mother's side whom I have never met and will probably never see again. My Chinese is embarrassing and they don't speak English—I forget names within seconds, syllables and tones snagged on the rugged banks of my mind like lichen lining the stone canals. One of the relatives is a local magistrate, finely dressed, tall and important-looking, not impressed by me or my Chinese-American family. He is the host of this very expensive multi-course meal in the private dining room of a government building in China—he will be the first to leave. The facts of our lives are offered, my mother introducing each member of my family. *This is my son-in-law—he has a golf academy. This is my daughter, she is a writer. This is their daughter and their two sons.* Later, when someone calls my children by their Chinese names, they don't respond—they don't know yet who they are. When lunch ends, I open a book purchased at the local bookshop. *Qingdao Old Constructions, Pen-and-Ink Drawings*—sketches of buildings, residences, villas, consulates, the old post office, the library. Everyone signs their name. Years later, this is all I will have left of them, signatures of lives that intersect, just barely, my own.

BACK TO SCHOOL

I am forty-eight and thinking about getting my master's degree. My best option is a low-residency program, one that requires me to be on campus once a year for ten days while I complete the rest of my coursework at home. Already I am stressed— who will be with my children when I'm gone? Is an advanced degree really necessary? Can we afford it? Will it make a difference for my career?

My friend J insists I look into her graduate program. I've never heard of it. I do an online search, consider several other schools, but they all present acute logistical nightmares. I don't have the bandwidth to find housing and food during the residency period, to coordinate with potential roommates, to navigate unfamiliar roads. J outlines the merits of her school. She talks about the department, the faculty and the ease in which she and her cohort progressed through the program. I send an email to the director and he responds in a matter of hours. The program is in Tacoma, Washington. I can catch a direct flight from Kona to Seattle on Alaska Airlines.

My mother lives in rural Graham, which I know is near Tacoma. I use Google Maps to see exactly how far away she is and blink at the results. Twenty-five minutes door to door from my mother's home to campus, twenty-nine if there's traffic.

I complete the application.

Like my father, my mother requires advance notice before a visit and, in her case, group approval for a visit since she lives in a communal environment. They're grateful for any translation help with sutras and make it clear that strictly social visits are denied though they have welcomed us multiple times. I have chanted and translated my way back into my mother's life but for some reason I don't tell her I have applied to a graduate school half an hour from her house. I will wait to see if I am accepted, and then tell her I am coming.

IN THE RED

The week before Easter, my friend J comes to Hawai'i as she does every year. I pick her up at the airport, having tanked up at Costco. We drive across the Big Island, west to east, to the volcano and Pele, the goddess who lives in Kīlauea, where we'll write for six days.

We stay in the Volcano Teapot Cottage. It's not in the shape of a teapot but it is owned by a couple, A and B. A is a retired nurse and English tea aficionado, B is a former Navy code breaker. The shelves are filled with teapots and teacups, their one acre of lush rainforest dotted with small figurines and broken china hidden amongst *hāpu'u* ferns. It has the quaint Victorian coziness one might expect from a bed and breakfast—a cast iron clawfoot tub, throw pillows with clever sayings like *It's Good to Be Queen* and *This is My Happy Place*. The fridge and freezer are stocked with essentials, every need considered down to individual pats of butter. In the mornings, B drops off fresh pastries.

There are two bedrooms, the master holding a queen-sized bed and the guest bedroom holding two twins. We alternate who stays where each visit, but it used to be a point of dissent. Who gets what. Who sleeps where. Who pays for what and who owes who. We have been friends for a long time, have watched our writing careers blossom and fade, then open again. There have been marriages, children. The last time she was here I applied for grad school, the same program she had attended, without telling my husband. He had joked/not joked as I stepped out the door that morning, "So what kind of trouble are you two going to get into this time?"

We alternate cooking dinner—breakfast and lunch are on our own. J is a vegetarian. We're both decent cooks, though with my family of five I'd rather not cook if I can avoid it. For this trip we coordinate our menus and I grab spices from my pantry at home—cumin, cayenne, paprika, red pepper flakes, cinnamon, curry powder, salmon rub. J is making an Asian stir fry one night so I add rice vinegar and soy sauce. I bring my cast iron pan to make eggs in hell.

We have an easy companionship now, though we've gone through periods where we stopped talking. I always dread this trip, at least in the weeks immediately before it, because it causes so much disruption for my family, so much extra work for me. J's boys are grown up—adult men, now—but I still have seventeen-, twelve- and nine-year-old children at home. Every time I say how hard it will be for me to get away, she tells me her life is hard, too. We've known each other for a long time, but I'm thinking we need a break from each other. I'm thinking this is the last year we'll be doing a writing getaway.

On our second day, I check my email and forward a message from a college admissions officer to my daughter, telling her to email the places she knows she won't be attending so they can offer the spot to someone else. A few hours later she texts me—*Mom. You sent that email to the admissions officer, too. Not just me and Dad. God!* I apologize and feel horrible.

That evening, I get another text from my daughter. *Where's the fucking paprika?!*

I text her back that I have it, and she freaks out. I tell her to go to the store and buy some, it's not the end of the world. She says she *just* got back from the store and she and her brothers are *starving* and she wanted to make some chicken since my husband is still at work. She continues to rant about "the fucking paprika," and when I point out she hasn't used it for a long time so how was I supposed to know she wanted it, she texts back icily, *I always cook when you're gone.*

This is what will later become known as The Fucking Paprika Incident, at least between me and a few writer friends I had been texting when all of this was going down. They love Maya's passion, they tell me, and a few "fucking paprika" jokes get tossed around.

But behind the humor I am secretly devastated. It's bad enough I'm not home, even worse I took the paprika. It's only March but this is my second trip away, and I'll leave again in four months for two weeks. My husband has trips planned to visit his father in California, but his absences don't wreak the kind of havoc mine do. My youngest usually cries, clinging to his father as I back out of the driveway. My son has told me before that he doesn't think mothers should be away from their children so much. Is it really that bad? Am I really that bad?

I am defiantly liberal with the paprika when I make the eggs in hell for dinner one night. J says it's amazing. I tell her I mashed two recipes together and was stressed because the oven temperature was off and I didn't want B to disrupt our schedule by coming over and tinkering with it. Also, I couldn't get the eggs to set so I had to use the broiler and was worried it might make the eggs rubbery. I tell her I was heavy handed with the paprika. I keep apologizing even as she asks me for the recipe. I don't know why I couldn't have just said thanks.

The next night I am up later than usual, agitated because my hormones are out of whack—my period is coming but I don't know when. It's past midnight when my daughter texts me.

> *R U up?*
> I text back. *Yes.*
> I can't call her since the cottage has thin walls and J is asleep. My daughter is trying to apply for a scholarship—it's due in the morning. She asks me

some questions about our finances that I can't answer because I'm not home. *You'll have to ask Dad*, I type. The next day she texts that she got up early—6:30 a.m. on a Saturday—but he had left to play a round of golf and the application is due at noon. I don't ask why she waited until the last minute to get this in— she applied for all of her scholarships and colleges on her own. My husband and I have let go of the reins because she seems to be in control and seems to know what she wants, but we forget she is still a kid.

I am miles away and don't have the answer she needs. *Text him*, I suggest. There's a pause before she types back, *I did*. We both know he may not respond for a while. We are both tired, having stayed up too late. There is nothing left to say.

A couple days later, she sends me pictures of her in her prom gown. It's a gorgeous, clingy thing of lace and scarlet red—we were at the outlet stores on Oʻahu but it still cost more money than she was willing to spend. "I'll get it," I told her, because it was beautiful on her and I wanted her to have this dress. We bought it months ago, and I had forgotten about it. She texts that she pinned it up but needs to sew it. Will I help?

I tell her of course. And then I tell her she looks lovely and that the dress is a lovely shade of paprika.

She texts back, apologizing for having freaked out. Then she texts, *but chicken needs paprika!* She says she and the boys were hungry and there was no food in the house. There was food in the house, of this I am sure—it was just not food they wanted to eat. But that's not the point. She'd gone to the store to buy chicken, excited to sprinkle some smoky paprika when she got back, and then came home and couldn't find it. So, yeah, she was disappointed. I tell her I need to write, but when I get home tomorrow I will help her with her dress and finish up her financial aid letters.

My writing benefits from these pockets of solitude, but at what cost? What is really at stake when I choose to leave? It's early when we pack up, gathering our clothes, the umbrellas, my printer, the paprika. We drive through the national park to give Pele a thank you and goodbye.

I cannot make up for my absences with my children. I accept that they are, in fact, may be what is called for at this juncture of family life.

As we drive across the island and to the airport, we talk about working together on a novel. We have some ideas, have told B to expect us again next year. I forgot this was supposed to be it, our last writing hurrah. "Sounds good," I say, because it does. At the curb, J waves goodbye.

VINE

On the way to a writing workshop, I curse the coordinator who thought it would be a good idea to house us in separate condos throughout Po'ipū, Kaua'i, "like pebbles scattered on a beach." My place is half a mile away from where we will be meeting, and there is a small hill, and it is hot. I am out of shape. I am not one who relishes the outdoors, who hikes through valleys or mucks through the rainforest, who breathes deep before plunging into the shimmering blue water of the Pacific. I am an air-conditioned sort of person, windblown only by a hair dryer, a woman whose road most travelled is between the desk in her bedroom and the kitchen.

· · ·

The map app announces the journey will take nine minutes, which means thirteen or fourteen minutes for me. The sun is full in the sky though it is not even 10:00 a.m. I trudge along the edge of the narrow road. Every so often a car passes a little too close. I am at the point in the walk where my head drops, even though it's only been ten minutes, and that's when I see, parallel to my path, a vine of heart-shaped leaves wending its way under fallen leaves and debris. Later, I will look it up: wild petunia, *Ipomoea obscura,* not native to Hawai'i, invasive. I lean over the guard rail to look for where it begins, but the vine goes on forever, heart after heart. I know better than to think this is a divine message.

· · ·

I walk this path for five days. On the last day, I pinch off a leaf and press it between the pages of my journal. When I find it weeks later, back at my bedroom desk with the air conditioner set at 79°F, the green has turned a mottled brown.

III.

In a time of destruction, create something.

THIS IS NOT A DRILL

JANUARY 13, 2018 – EMERGENCY ALERT – 8:07 A.M.
BALLISTIC MISSLE THREAT INBOUND TO HAWAII.
SEEK IMMEDIATE SHELTER. THIS IS NOT A DRILL.

8:07 a.m. When our phones simultaneously chime throughout the house, I am talking to my mother on the phone about my younger brother who hasn't spoken to me in several years. My daughter has a swim meet and tells us to look at the message, *like right now,* and then asks, "Um, is this for real?" My husband is on his way to play golf and wants to know if he should cancel. My sons are playing on their devices—the youngest has his headphones on.

8:12 a.m. When we decide the alert is real, or real enough, we start stockpiling water. My husband fills the tubs, I fill the washer. My daughter gathers everyone's closed-toe shoes—*no slippers,* I tell her. I take out our passports and cash, I text a cousin on the island who isn't perturbed by the alert in the slightest. My older son closes all the windows. My youngest slips off his headphones. "What's going on?" he asks. "Nothing," we tell him. He shrugs and puts his headphones back on.

8:15 a.m. What we don't do: we don't hug, we don't cry, we don't huddle in the center of our house. We don't pray, though if ever there was a time for prayer, this would be it. We don't say goodbye, we don't call our family on the mainland. I think, briefly, about breaking out a board game. We could die playing Monopoly, or Life, or Sorry! But we don't actually think we are going to die. Do we?

8:18 a.m. What we do when we've done all we can: we wait.

8:20 a.m.

8:23 a.m.

8:27 a.m.

8:31 a.m.

8:33 a.m.

8:34 a.m.

8:35 a.m.

8:39 a.m.

8:42 a.m.

8:44 a.m.

8:45 a.m.

THERE IS NO MISSILE THREAT OR DANGER TO THE
STATE OF HAWAII. REPEAT. FALSE ALARM.

8:46 a.m. We return to our lives. I get back on the phone. My husband goes to the golf course. The boys keep playing on their devices. My daughter drives to the swim meet where she will beat her best time and place for states, the first time ever.

A few friends call from the mainland—*Oh my God, are you all right?* I laugh it off. *Crazy, right?*

Later I would start buying emergency supplies from Amazon.

Later I would go to Facebook and see what other people did—dove off the side of their boats into the water, dropped their children into manholes and sewer drains, barricaded themselves in their bathrooms with pots and pans over their heads.

Later I would break down—nerves shot, adrenals shot—and cry to my therapist.

Later I would look at the screen shot I took of the alert, and see the notification that appeared right below it, from an app called 5-Minute Journal.

Good morning! Ready to start your day with gratitude?

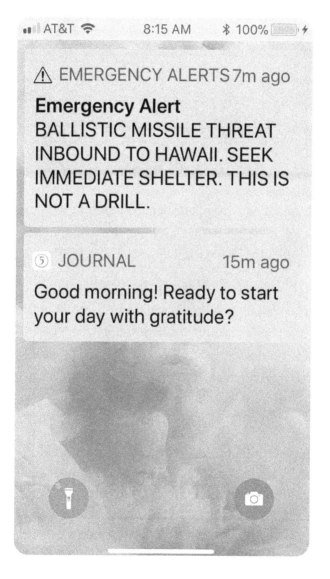

ON WATCHING THE DOG
WE GET THREE TIMES
A WEEK

This morning I stood at the kitchen window
and watched our part-time dog work the marrow
of a bone. He buried it in our backyard, then

dug it up, covered in dirt and grit. He carried it
in his mouth like an egg about to be cracked.
He traveled to all four corners of the property,

a ferryman across grass and rock, stopping
under the shade of a banana tree. His paws
turned loose the earth and I saw it disappear,

dropped into a temporary safe house, a hidden
earthen chamber. Some bones will be found—
we know this. By my husband, the gardener,

the children. Turned over by the lawnmower
or dug up by the neighbor's dog who roams
our yard without a leash.

No matter.
There are more treasures waiting.
There are more wanting to be found.

TAKE 30 WITH FOOD

My mother had heart failure last week. She told me as an afterthought, having twice said, *I'm fine now,* but I didn't understand so I asked, *What's fine now?* Thirty pounds of water weight, difficulty breathing, an irregular heartbeat. Her bookshelf now cluttered with bottles of Chinese herbs rolled into small, black balls. *Take 30 with food.* Stinky teas and poultices to press against a wound, needles as thin as a hair or thick as a nail, they quiver when they break the skin. It happened after my uncle died. She watched his funeral on the computer, beamed in terabytes across the country, ended up in an emergency room that night. She turned eighty while in the hospital. *This was practice,* she told me. *So I'll be ready when the time comes.* Her nephew, her father, her mother, her older brother. Every death reveals something new. Colon cancer kept secret (two uncles), high cholesterol, high blood pressure, lousy hearts, blood in the bowels, a lazy eye, ears that won't stop ringing. When I update my medical history with the click of a mouse, my Western doctor tells me to come in for more tests. My Chinese doctor covers my back with glass jars and swirling smoke. I tell myself I will be immune, my Americanness will save me. I eat kale, rub bio-identical progesterone on my skin, meditate with an app on my iPhone. My pantry is filled with plastic bins of vitamins, some so large I have to cut them in two. At night I run my hands over my body, repeat affirmations, wonder what it will take to change my own history.

ODE TO THE SPAM MUSUBI

Those of us who weren't local were skeptical. Carby, fatty, and what kind of meat was Spam, anyway? Why not steamed chicken, quinoa, kale? One bite and we were sunk. We bought plastic molds to make the perfect musubi—a sheet of dried seaweed, a page from the ocean torn in half. A layer of steamed rice. A slice of Spam, lightly fried, maybe brushed with oyster sauce, maybe not. Stacked three inches high, an edible Lego building block of white and pink.

The aunties knew the way to a child's heart at every soccer game. When my daughter leaves Hawai'i and heads for the mainland, cans of Spam at the grocery store remind her of home. A plate of unexpected musubis at an Asian restaurant might bring tears. Because, Spam musubi, you are an unexpected lifeline, the salty sweet of my children's youth. How many times have you have saved us when the kids were melting down? There, stacked in a pyramid by the register of the gas station. There, under the heat lamps at the Sack N Save, the warm weight a bean bag waiting to be tossed into the mouths of fractious children. I sing the merits of potted meats wrapped in rice, sealed with a strip of seaweed wrapped tight like a ribbon around a present.

SOME DAYS I JUST WANT TO WEAR OLD UNDERWEAR

I don't mean underwear that is dirty or has been sitting on top of the hamper, waiting for its turn in the laundry. I mean underwear with shot elastic, the cotton worn thin, small rips or tears. The ones shoved in the back of the drawer that you can't throw away, because *just in case*. Good underwear can be expensive. You can buy a three-pack at the big box stores, but it always feels like you're scrimping. Then again, when I look at the lacy options laid out like a dessert buffet on glass tables at a department store, each one costing an hour of minimum wage, I think, *yeah, no*. Sometimes the old underwear is a little tight, a size or two too small. With everything that is happening, I've gained a little weight. I bought new underwear online. When they arrived, I tried them on. They were comfortable. I washed them and then bought more. But this morning I rose from my bed and made the mistake of checking my phone. I read the news. I read some emails. When I went to get dressed, I could only dig around for my old underwear. Even holding it in my hand felt like a relief. That some things never change.

That some things stay the same. When I pulled them on, it didn't matter that they were tight, cutting into my soft belly. They were familiar. I still remembered.

INTERPRETATIONS

Dream. I am in the guest room at the top of the stairs. The room is spare and simple—I am its only occupant even though I am married with three children. The bed is simply made with sheets and a thin, nubby cotton blanket. There is a slim bureau and a small side table with a single lamp. There is no desk—my laptop rests on my lap. I have no luggage, no suitcase. The room is windowless.

I am working on a book, a collection of narratives about the women in my mother's maternal line, specifically the women I consider to be my grandfather's three wives. My grandmother is, by my count, wife number two.

A few doors down, past the stairs, is another room. It's filled with things that people cannot find a place for in the house—extra towels and bedsheets, old books and newspapers, photo albums and mementos. Clothes are crammed into the closet on mismatched hangers. Much of what is here has been discarded and forgotten—the overage, the worn, the outgrown, the just-in-case.

A printer sits on a rickety rosewood table with a glass top. I recognize this table because it was in my childhood house—there is a chip in the bottom left corner of the glass. I don't question why it is here, because of course it would be here. This is the family house. Evidence of my life is everywhere.

The cover of the printer is open, the ink cartridge displaced. The lighted display flashes—PRINT JOB INCOMPLETE. My manuscript rests in the output tray. Each page has the title of my book at the top, printed on both sides, the pages fanned from having been stacked on one another unevenly. *Other Small Histories.* I wonder who might have seen this. I wonder who opened the cover of the printer and removed the ink cartridge.

My grandmother must know what I have done. If she suspected me before, she is certain now—I am telling family secrets, writing them down for the world to see. Perhaps the relatives are discussing it at this moment, gathered in the kitchen with steaming cups of tea, speaking in low whispers. *Disrespectful girl. So American, so thoughtless. To have written without permission or consideration, and for what? What good is dragging up the past? Where are her loyalties? So impulsive. So selfish.* They cluck their tongues, shake their heads.

I do not think of defending myself, nor do I think about leaving this house. I do not think of anything other than *they are not happy* and *I have told these stories.* The two are interconnected and not mutually exclusive.

Perhaps I misread the pursed lips of my grandmother when she told me goodnight—instead of disapproval, could it have been resignation, even relief? The pages hadn't been destroyed but someone wanted me to know they had been seen.

I return the ink cartridge to the printer. I snap the lid closed. The printer churns back to life, spitting out one final page, the last page of my manuscript.

I gather the pages in my arms and hold them against my chest.

I wake up.

WHILE YOU WERE ON AN IMPORTANT ZOOM MEETING

Call me asap
MOM
MOM
MOM
I HOPE YOUR COMPUTER IS DINGING
CALL ME
CALL ME
CALL ME
ASAP
ASAP
MOM
MOM
MOM
ANSWER THE PHONE
Where are you
I need you
And you're not answering

TRESPASSES

This morning someone put rat poison in the empty field behind our house. On my own, I wouldn't have recognized it, the small aquamarine crystals glittering like amulets, something you might find strung on a bracelet or lining the bottom of a fish aquarium, a pirate's chest nearby.

Some of the neighborhood dogs—a border collie; an American pitbull; our own part-time poi dog, black as night—sniffed at the scattered piles with interest before we knew what it was. A couple hours later, one of the dogs was rushed to the vet. The neighborhood dog owners went up in arms. Calls were made. Social media alerts were posted. The development company that owned the land said it wasn't their poison, but no one believed them. Small clusters of people, unmasked, conversed in angry whispers on our street corner.

As part-time dog owners, we were reluctant to take sides. Our house bordered this land. We had complained of mosquitos breeding in the discarded tractor tires, of kids tagging the cement blocks, of drug deals and secret trysts revealing a tangle of limbs if you looked close. The field was not public land. It was private, the NO TRESPASSING signs long torn down, but everyone knew. We did not want to get involved. I said this several times, then gave up and went to take pictures so I could file a report.

Someone stood alone in the wide expanse of the field, shoveling the poison into a bucket. How can I fairly describe this man? Elderly, retired, not from Hawai'i but wearing a dark baseball hat with the University of Hawai'i logo. When we first moved in, he would stand in the field above our house, looking down into our kitchen while we sat eating dinner. He walked his dog along our property line—more than once it growled at us. He often commented on our yard. *I don't know what you're trying to do, but I don't think that's going to work.* He had a tetchy look on his face whenever we passed him on the street. We were fairly sure he voted for Trump. But when I saw him bent over, all seventy-five years of him and a bit on the heavy side, I thought I could probably lighten up. A hurricane was coming.

We were in the middle of a global pandemic, and on most days I felt like the worst that could happen was already happening, but it would turn out I was wrong. It was, after all, 2020. I decided to be kind. I thanked him for cleaning up. I was standing too close, so I backed up. I wished him luck this weekend, when the hurricane was due to hit. He said they would be fine. *But*, he added, *you'd better take those chairs down.* He pointed to five teak chairs that sat at the top of our property. I told him we would, and left.

AND NOW THE WATTLE

That I have to look up the spelling
for *wattle* tells you I don't really
know what I am dealing with.

I was brushing my hair, mesmerized
by the shiny silver strands that have
made themselves known since this

pandemic began and then I turned,
a bit too quick, to glance at the side
mirror and that's when I saw it, the

soft pocket of flesh below my chin.
I blinked several times, unsure
of what I was seeing. I brushed

my teeth, did exercises with my jaw—
it did not go away. The opposite
of a landing pad, it is a place where

things begin. Or, possibly, where things
end. After all—gravity. Things can only
go down from here.

PHOTOGRAPH: ( )

Picture this: a train platform in Taipei, March 2011. My parents sitting side by side, my father clad in a sporty bright red North Face jacket, my mother with an army-green handkerchief tied around her head. Their eyes cast down as they each read a novel, covers prominent, a Hallmark commercial for aging parents absorbed in your creative work. Absorbed may be too strong a word, though they tell me they are proud of me. I am not prepared for this and fumble my thank you. They read as we wait for a train to take us to Xiangde Temple in Hualien, three hours south of the city, to see the thirty-six-foot gold statue of Ksitigarbha, the bodhisattva my mother has studied and paid homage to for over thirty years. On the train, they will sit together. My seat, reversed, will face them—they are my only view. What else is there to say? They are still legally married. They file joint tax returns, have joint bank accounts. They lead separate lives but see each other a couple of times a year. They email. They have an easy companionship now, and I am inserting myself into this moment, having left my own young family in Hawai'i. I will extend my stay from three weeks to two months, unable to leave. On this trip my mother will introduce me to the custard apple, its seeded flesh creamy and sweet. My father will take me to a celebration in honor of my Aunt I-An, near some famous hot springs, where she will be asked to play the harmonica. For many mornings, my father and I will have breakfast at a local restaurant as my mother studies with her Buddhist group—my father will read the Chinese newspaper, breaking *yóutiáo* into his salted soybean soup. Later, at a local hospital, he will be wheeled away to have stents put in to prop open his arteries. My mother and I will complete the paperwork, wait for the surgery to be over. She will pray, I will fret. In the end, he is fine. Years later, when my mother sends an email telling me she is once again proud of me, I flush a furious red even though we are thousands of miles apart. When my father sends me a picture on WeChat and tells me his friend cut his hair, I say, *it looks good, I hope you are well, I love you.* I wonder how much longer I will have them. I wonder what else still needs to be said.

BACKYARD

It's June 2020 and thanks to the pandemic, we are quarantined. My husband is gardening. He's up early before the sun makes it too hard to work.

We don't have much by way of soil—it's more dirt and rock—so we've had deliveries of the rich, brown stuff, smelling faintly of manure. When the invoice comes I tell myself it's cheaper than therapy.

He's been furloughed for three months and was just told it would be extended three more. In our state, he's lucky to be furloughed—most people were laid off, no benefits, no hope of returning to a job they might have loved. He had been wary when he started, not sure if it was a fit, skeptical of his co-workers, but then work became something important, relevant, enjoyable. He was promoted, then promoted again. He was in line for another promotion this month.

So, it was a blow.

Meanwhile, our part-time dog is eating the long blades of grass in the field beyond our house, chewing with the resigned tentativeness of a child faced with a bowl of vegetables. We worry he might be sick, or have an upset stomach, or hosting some kind of parasite.

Everything is *or*. That's what this time has become, terror and fear over things big and small. His owner tells us it's normal, but we watch him, just in case.

Ralph Waldo Emerson said a weed is a plant whose virtues are undiscovered. Our dirt plot seems to be full of them, weeds that thrive without water or decent pH. Weeds that withstand the dry heat of USDA Hardiness Zone 12a, our tropical savanna according to the Köppen climate classification. They are indifferent to the wind which can be relentless on some days, driving the humans indoors. The weeds always seem to find a way.

The last big purchase my husband made was for fifty strips of sod, each the size of a doormat, for the small terrace he dug out of the hill. I woke to the sound of shovel hitting rock, morning after morning. On the day he rolled out the thick strips of grass, our dirt terrace became a carpet of velvet green. He dropped to his knees, then fell on his back, gaze to the sky, arms outstretched. The kids and I stayed in the house, watching him through the curtains. For a second, it seemed as if he had fallen asleep. Then we saw his chest rise, his small breaths.

The next time our part-time dog comes over, my husband shows him the new grass. The dog is not so sure. He sniffs cautiously before taking a step. He knows this wasn't here before and yet here it is, permanent and real. Alive. The seams where one strip joins the next are barely visible—in some places you can't see where one ends and another begins. It will take at least a month to become a single expanse of grass, the only uninterrupted green on our dirt hill. It will seem as if it's always been this way, this tiny oasis, the roots reaching through the earth in search of water.

A NOTE FROM ME TO THE KIDS

Please cook the fucking greens that are wilting in the fridge and while you are at it, empty the dishwasher, sweep the floors, vacuum the bedrooms. Get rid of the dust on the windowsills, the hard water stains on the bathroom sink. Wash some clothes, fold the towels in thirds the way I showed you. Take out the recyclables. Fill the water bottles, wipe the smudges from the microwave door. Some days it feels like life is going to hell in a laundry basket. I mean, the empty toilet paper roll. Really? But other days—well. Other days I'm grateful. Other days I remember there are worse things, that some children don't come home. That the body can be in constant pain. That more of my ancestors have had it worse compared with those who've had it better. This life, in contrast, is a delight. So help me out, kids. There is so much to do.

SOUS

Our evening meal is prepared on rotation—my husband times three, my eldest son and daughter each times two. The youngest one holds domain over the dishes and I, according to the schedule taped to the refrigerator, no longer cook dinner. Still, I try to help. I make two types of salsa to accompany the chicken tamales my son is steaming in the rice cooker. "Sure," he says when I offer. "If you want to." I find bulbs of shallots forgotten in the back of the fridge, tender beneath their papery skins. A jar of flaccid jalapeños. Cherry tomatoes the size of ping pong balls, still on the vine. A trio of small, sweet peppers. Frozen pineapple chunks from the remains of school lunches, packed in to-go containers picked up daily for the last two months of school, drive-through style, all of us wearing masks. Cilantro from the garden, even though the plant has bolted. A grind of sea salt. A squeeze of lime juice that doesn't want to come out, no matter how hard I roll that small jade stone. I use my manual food processor with the bright red lid, pulling a little too enthusiastically to chop everything up—the tomatoes foam in protest. The pineapple salsa ends up spicy even though I only added three small slices of jalapeño, no seeds. At dinner, my fourteen-year old son, the chef, takes a spoonful of each, a nimbus of color on his plate. "Wow," he says. "It's good, Mom." I was holding my breath. I was worried it might not be enough.

ARTIFACT

1.

I have a brother, two years and three months younger than me. For a long time we didn't really have much to say to each other. And then we did. And then we didn't.

2.

Our father was a geophysicist, which meant he looked at geologic formations and tried to figure out what they meant, what was in and under them. He was finishing his PhD at Washington University in St. Louis when I was born, and then took a job with an oil company in Houston where my brother was born.

3.

Both my brother and I went to boarding school. My father had been transferred many times and now we were living overseas in Hong Kong while the company searched for oil in the South China Sea. They would pay for us to study back in the US. I went to an all-girls boarding school in Connecticut, he went to a coed boarding school in Massachusetts. A few years later, we would flip flop—I would go to college in Massachusetts while he transferred to a new school in Connecticut.

4.

The study of geology and geophysics is the study of the earth. You use gravitational, magnetic and seismic methods to figure out the earth's internal structure, its evolution. Rifts, continental sutures, mid-oceanic ridges. Earthquakes. Volcanoes.

5.

My brother and I don't really know each other. I can say that now, looking back at what we had and what we didn't. We have some things in common—I hold onto this. We both love Baskin Robbins' Jamoca Almond Fudge. We both bite our nails. We are perfectionists, we are hard on ourselves, we can be obsessive, we have a temper.

6.

What is important to him now? Did I ever really know? What are his passions, his bucket list, his thoughts about religion? I wonder if he thinks about death. I just turned fifty and for the past couple of years, that's all I could think about. I wonder if he worries about it like I do.

7.

Geophysics is fundamental to the needs of society. It's how we find energy, water, mineral resources. It's how we monitor environmental impacts. It's how we assess natural and manmade hazards.

8.

I can't tell you why my brother and I no longer talk. As people like to say, it's complicated. It's not just about us, but about people we love. We have our allegiances. There's no way getting around it.

9.

A few years ago, my father told me I was the one who needed to fix things. I bristled. I had already apologized multiple times, though I wasn't sure what I was apologizing for anymore. That might have been the problem. I tried to tell my father it wasn't just me, but he couldn't hear me. *Fix it,* he said.

10.

I apologized again. I still couldn't fix it.

11.

I admit I am attached to an idea of our relationship, a kind of hologram that had been thrown up for my viewing pleasure in the few years we were together. I created a story that might have been flawed—I was its only author. That's not to say what we had wasn't real. We cared about each other—I tell myself we still do. In our own way.

12.

From my parents, I sneak the occasional picture. My brother is in good shape, relatively healthy, a non-smoker, not diabetic, in his late forties. I hear from him for the first time in years when he has heart failure. The email begins with *Hi*. He doesn't call me by name. When he signs off, it is just his first initial. He writes that doctors were shocked he had managed daily activities for six days after his heart started to give out. *You have a strong heart with limited blood flow*, they told him. We have that in common, too.

13.

I write him back.
He never replies.

14.

Fractures are the dominant mechanism of rock failure when studying the physical and mechanical behavior of rock mass. It impacts how we deal with the exploration of natural resources, it affects engineering projects and the prediction of earthquakes. They are sometimes called faults. But fractures have their place—they allow for movement. I can live with that.

PROVIDENCE

On the side of the road near our home on the hill in Waimea, a cluster of perfumed yellow ginger, *Hedychium flavescens,* also known as cream garland-lily or *'awapuhi melemele.*

I know what this is like, the many names one can be called.

. . .

We always want to be something we're not. So many times, I wished I was white. I would look in the mirror at my Chinese face staring back at me, willing myself to be different.

. . .

In Hawai'i, yellow ginger is everywhere but is non-native to this place. Its home is in the Himalayas, and also southwest China, Sichuan province, though I don't remember seeing it when I was there. Funny what you miss when you're not looking.

. . .

My children wish they had Hawaiian blood. Being born and raised here isn't enough—they have no claim to this place they call home. It's hard when you don't know where you belong.

. . .

Yellow ginger grows wild in the Islands. The oval flower head, or "spike," has overlapping green bracts in multiple spiral rows, with yellow flowers. You can't eat yellow ginger—it's ornamental, strung or woven into leis.

. . .

Growing up, I felt pitted against other Asian Americans, all of us proving our worthiness. In China, I wasn't Chinese enough. In Hawai'i, I got to unlearn all of that. I hope my kids will, too.

. . .

It's easy to confuse yellow ginger with other kinds of ginger. Shampoo ginger, edible ginger, white ginger, *kāhili* ginger. To the untrained eye, it's possible to see how they all look alike, to assume they are the same, so similar that distinction may not seem necessary.

It is.

ACKNOWLEDGMENTS

My thanks to the team at Watermark Publishing, George Engebretson and Dawn Sakamoto, who said yes to the idea of a guided memoir line and became my partners in making the Hali'a Aloha series a reality. Dawn, we are overdue for drinks on this one.

Mahalo to the friends and family who make my day-to-day life as a parent and writer easier: Lavonne Leong, Mary Spears, Jessica Barksdale, Christina Wong, Kim Rogers, Lorna Saito, Starr Anastasio and Akamai, our part-time dog. To Marcelo Hernandez Castillo for graciously allowing me to use the first three lines of his poem, "Cenzontle." To Rigoberto González, Suzanne Berne and Rick Barot for guiding me to this work and helping me stay the course. To my parents, who willingly answer my many questions as I continue to understand my past. To my children—Maya, Eric and Luke: I know it can be tough having a mom who's also a writer. Thank you for hanging in there with me, I love you. To my husband, Darrin, who reads multiple drafts of every book and continues to be my most loyal fan and cheerleader. *This is exactly the kind of life I want to be living, and with you.*

To the island of Hawai'i, which helped me bring three humans into the world and gave me gentle permission to start writing again. I am grateful.

PUBLICATION NOTES

Grateful acknowledgement is made to the editors of the following journals for publishing earlier versions of the following work:

CALYX Journal: "Lullaby" and "Banquet" (both of which also appear in my chapbook, *Other Small Histories,* published by the Poetry Society of America)

Columbia Journal: "At the American Chamber of Commerce Dinner in Beijing (1995)"

Poetry Northwest: "Take 30 With Food"

DARRIN GEE

Darien Hsu Gee is the author of five novels published by Penguin Random House that have been translated into eleven languages. She won the 2019 Poetry Society of America's Chapbook Fellowship award for *Other Small Histories* and the 2015 Hawai'i Book Publishers' Ka Palapala Po'okela Award of Excellence for *Writing the Hawai'i Memoir*. She is the recipient of a Sustainable Arts Foundation grant and a Vermont Studio Center fellowship. Gee holds a B.A. from Rice University and an M.F.A. from the Rainier Writing Workshop at Pacific Lutheran University. She lives with her family on the Big Island of Hawai'i.

dariengee.com

CPSIA information can be obtained
at www.ICGtesting.com
Printed in the USA
LVHW012331210221
679514LV00007B/816